Dedicated to the sojourners

Ark House Press
arkhousepress.com

Beauty Maker
Copyright Sarah Alison 2024

All writing is permissible to share by readers across all social platforms if the writer is credited / Sarah Alison

All rights reserved. No part of this publication may be reproduced or transmitted by any person or entity, in any form or by any means. This includes photocopying, recording and scanning without prior permission from the author and publisher. This book is not permitted for resale/wholesale unless a direct agreement has been made with the author.

978-0-9756331-3-7 (pbk)

Cover Art: Kaye Redman kayeredman.com @kayeredmanart	Editors and Encouragers: Lauren Steffes www.consecrate.co @consecrateco
Layout: Sarah Alison sarahalison.com.au @sarahalison	Lacey Shelton Christine Willard

Visit Sarah at sarahalison.com.au
or follow along on Instagram: @sarahalison

Scripture quotations marked NIV are taken from the Holy Bible, New International Version®, NIV®, Copyright © 1973, 1978, 1984, 2011 by Biblica, Inc.® Used by permission. All rights reserved worldwide.

Scripture quotations marked TPT are from The Passion Translation®. Copyright © 2017, 2018 by Passion & Fire Ministries, Inc. Used by permission. All rights reserved. ThePassionTranslation.com.

Scripture quotations taken from the Amplified® Bible (AMP), Copyright © 2015 by The Lockman Foundation. Used by permission. lockman.org

Eternal thanks to the bouquet of fragrant women who have arrived in my life right on time, for such a time as this, to wrestle with the Word, receive conviction, rely on Christ's strength in our weakness, and spur one other on towards Beauty.

BEAUTY MAKER
Finding Grace in the
Light of Surrender

CONFUSION // PAGE 7

SURRENDER // PAGE 51

BEAUTY // PAGE 103

BLESSING // PAGE 167

STORIES // PAGE 197

Beauty Maker was birthed through dreams and visions, of waking up right on the tick of midnight with words I had never heard before, unravelling revelations, dreams about paragraphs of words that my pen found as the sun arose, and notes I felt to give to friends that bounded back to me in discovery.

They've come from learnings that have opened my eyes wider and wider as I continued the daily habit of searching His Word as treasure and filling my mind with what was pure and true and lovely alongside like-minded hearts.

They came as histories of previous God-glories, reminding me of the wonders that honest prayers and heartfelt praises made way for—all pieces to the puzzle, messages to gird me, to strengthen me, and to pass onto others.

This process has felt like walking uphill—not easy—and sometimes seemingly far too steep for my clumsy legs. But I have sensed the hand of God guiding me, teaching me, and being so very patient as I stumbled over my own boulders. God has given me respite and encouragement all the way.

Time to order my thoughts in the still, quiet place has been hard to claim, as the call to raise five small children and keep order in the home continues to ring loud. I wonder if that's why God has used the less-than-usual amount of disjointed sleep with a baby in the quiet hours of midnight to speak to me. It has all been a grace.

As you read these words, may you trek through the rugged terrain with Him, too—handing over the burdens on your back and holding fast to the truth of His presence and help.

Let's keep going, for there is much beauty in the making.

CONFUSION

REFINEMENT THROUGH THE FIRE—GOING BACK TO ANSWER THE
BASIC QUESTIONS YOU THOUGHT YOU KNEW BUT NOW HAVE TO LIVE

THIS IS THE BREAKING UP OF FALLOW GROUND

BEAUTY MAKER

Where is hope when darkness blankets me?
Where is faith when confusion is all I see?

It was washed away in that reckless, tormenting sea,
leaving behind only buckets of stormy grief.

I'll wander down to the river,
where the water lies serene.
I'll sit; I'll kneel. I'll pour it all out to Him,
letting this dark storm be captured by the stream.

Desperate hands will cast out line,
pull in far-off hope, and slowly,
let Him replace my grief with His peace.

The waters—they can give life and take it away,
a true mystery that I seek to convey.
I'll wander down to the river and let Jesus heal me.

CONFUSION

The healing of a broken heart starts with the rise of an honest song of lament and ends with getting out of the driver's seat and letting grace drive you to the place where you finally hear those beautiful words of love—

"Let me heal you."

BEAUTY MAKER

The winds that once beckoned me out of safety to follow their sweet-loving scent up steep mountain paths now kindly close the doors, and I find myself soul-deep in the wine press, treading new oil around and around this same old mill.

Daylight hours stretch wide, but here, my eyes, searching for beauty in the beige, hear Him sing about a new adventure coming in pastel sunset hues.

As the sun disappears over the horizon, the rain shimmers purple and forms a river through my garden, and I bathe in its promise.

I laugh with the stars and mourn with them too, and wait for His promise that the doors will open soon.

CONFUSION

Fire falls from the clouds
And lands in the distance,
But up above still echoes loud.

I won't run after counterfeit treasure,
I'll fly after the source above
To discover its full grandeur.

When I reach the blaze, I have a choice–
Do I dare trek down that unknown path?
And listen to the Refiner's Fire's voice?

Yes, I will choose to dance through,
Dare to surrender my imperfections,
Allowing my spirit to move.

I'll find joy in the flames,
Singing my songs of love,
And loudly declaring His praise.

I'll reach the blazing garden-heart,
After the heat has done its work–
Refined, but not marked.

I'll make home with the Living Word,
Feast continually on His goodness,
And drink the new wine He's poured.

BEAUTY MAKER

I don't want to tip-toe around my shortcomings any longer.

I want to confront them and ask them where they came from. Then I'll get on my knees, bring my sin into the Light of day, and turn from my ways.

My shortcomings do not disqualify me. They keep me reliant on grace.

CONFUSION

The sea was restless; the waves grew weary. The fog fell thick, and the darkness lingered.

I was determined not to give in to the sounds of the night until the safe hands of steady ground held me in place.

Perseverance was my paddle.

My eyes—squinting through it all, searched for the Lighthouse. My ears—blocking out every taunting sound, listened only to Hope's faint whisper.

It was clear, yet quiet.
I felt lost, yet certain.
I was getting closer.

BEAUTY MAKER

Logos is language in action. Where eternal became temporal and infinite became finite. Logos is the Living Word, ultimate truth, and divine wisdom. He manifested Himself into creation to bring redemption and is not bound by the past, present, or future but is the beginning and the end. He is no longer hidden behind curtains for 'special,' religious people but is available to you and me. Logos is speaking now. May our ears be opened to hear Him.

CONFUSION

Taking time to really chew on the words matters just as much as eating them.

Selah.

For the word of God is alive and active. Sharper than any double-edged sword, it penetrates even to dividing soul and spirit, joints and marrow; it judges the thoughts and attitudes of the heart.

Hebrews 4:12 NIV

CONFUSION

If you desire wisdom, the eternal wisdom that existed before the world began, before the dust, the wisdom whose very breath created us, the wisdom that became a man and whose message was Truth—look at what He has made.

Go back to the Garden. Pay attention to what lives there and how it lives. Consider the lilies of the field. Learn from the planting and the harvest. Watch a seed grow and bloom and die and multiply. Look at the trees. Witness the seasons. Pay attention.

Listen to the poetry He has written in the Garden for us to behold every single day. Truth is found there.

BEAUTY MAKER

Melody's Garden

Dust was where we began, but Your nail-scarred hands scattered seeds.

Your arms brought Living Water to heal the earth of its barrenness.

Here, Your knees kissed the depths of our souls as You worked the ground, planting roses in the soil of sorrow.

Your heart hurt along with ours, but Your presence filled us with songs of hope beyond it all.

You planted faith in me, and You planted faith in Melody. Her journey home reminded us all that dust is where we all began, and it's where we will all return.

But the fragrance of her journey remains, along with all of the songs she sang. Her life and love still point us to You.

We know you are faithful to make beauty, even from ashes.

Jesus answered, "I am the way and the truth and the life. No one comes to the Father except through me."

John 14:6 NIV

BEAUTY MAKER

I remember a girl who once dared to hope to be a mother. For five years, she chose to dream again and again, even in the midst of the pain it caused her when she never saw her dream fulfilled. She almost gave up, but Heaven's hand lifted her up and gave her strength to hope yet again.

Her hope was at its highest, but then it brought her to her lowest when the answer sounded once again like 'no.' It is a moment tattooed forever like a battle scar across her heart while she was there on her knees, falling apart.

She left a lake of tears at her feet that day. But she didn't sweep it away. Instead, she sat in its solace and dared to ask, 'why?'

The reply was always, 'Trust Me.'

And on that Easter Friday, she did. She trusted. Like she imagined those witnesses had, too, on the first Easter Friday when they thought all hope was lost. She hoped that God would redeem her story and turn it for His good.

The scar still remains. But instead of telling a story of pain, it now tells a story of hope.

Eight Easters later, she remembered the scarred hands of God Himself who came to meet that girl at her lake of sorrow and weep with her. Except on that same day, she was now anticipating the arrival of baby number five.

Praise be to the God and Father of our Lord Jesus Christ, the Father of compassion and the God of all comfort, who comforts us in all our troubles, so that we can comfort those in any trouble with the comfort we ourselves receive from God.

2 Corinthians 1:3-4 NIV

BEAUTY MAKER

It all started in the secret place.

Quietly, Beauty Himself chose,
with a deep desire to love *you*,
to come, divinely and silently,
to the womb of a young virgin.

He unclothed Himself of His glory,
and came as the seed of God.
He took on the flesh of His creation.
He took on fragility instead of power
and began unravelling His plan of redemption.

That single moment,
in all of its gentle humility
is enough to take the air
completely out of the lungs
and draw the body to the ground
in deep relief.

But He planned on going even further still—
His glory, His beauty, His power,
ripped, scorned, hated
and nailed to death.

He knew.

CONFUSION

He knew this was the path He had to take.
For in taking on our flesh,
He planned to take on our sin
and brokenness, too.

The seed of God died
in every way,
from conception onwards,
in order to reap a great harvest.

And with it came an invitation for *you*
to rise from your knees
and stand side-by-side
with Jesus, our beautiful Saviour,
to die with Him,
to surrender everything to Him,
to hide yourself in Him,
with His seed also hidden within you,
and reap a harvest—one hundredfold—
because of Him.

It all starts in the secret place.

BEAUTY MAKER

Reading can be like choosing whom we want to be mentored by, but we get to choose from *anyone* in any era who felt the pull to put their thoughts, stories, and lessons onto paper. We even get to choose from all of the lifetimes before ours. There is much to learn, but we *must* choose wisely.

CONFUSION

The wisdom of the Word surpasses
the wisdom of the world.

Every time.

BEAUTY MAKER

In times of confusion, when answers are nowhere in sight, questions feel like echoes at midnight, and prayers sound like whispers in a storm—here the seeds of your faith get the opportunity to not just know Truth but to truly live it.

Here, the radicle root—that very first hidden growth reaching into the soil, slowly becomes the foundation of radical faith.

Lord, my heart is meek before you. I don't consider myself better than others. I'm content to not pursue matters that are over my head—such as your complex mysteries and wonders—that I'm not yet ready to understand. I am humbled and quieted in your presence. Like a contented child who rests on its mother's lap, I'm your resting child, and my soul is content in you.

Psalms 131:1-2 TPT

BEAUTY MAKER

I will not be able to rejoice in this day
if I do not first gladly accept
the challenges that it will bring.

This day holds unseen wonders
and heavenly treasures.
But if my mind is holding onto
where it falls short,
where I fall short,
a cloak of grey covers over it all.

Accepting my limitations today,
letting grace fill in all my cracks,
allows my eyes to glimpse
a world beyond this one,
where my surrender is the shovel,
and grace is the trove.

Let us dig.

CONFUSION

Take heart, cocooned one.

These hidden days are the foundations of the beauty that you are becoming.

All you are learning here is being formed with detail onto your new, glorious wings.

Take heart, faithful one, and keep singing. Soon you will take flight.

BEAUTY MAKER

Some trees make home near the ocean, swaying with the sea.

Some trees are planted in secret gardens, only to be looked upon by those who trek their hidden paths. Some grow slowly, blooming pretty through autumn, never late, but always on time. Some seem to struggle in their soil and almost lose to the ravages of the earth. Some sadly do not make it.

Some stretch tall and reach the stars, while others reach out, holding hands with other branches. Some trees grow both tall and wide, providing comfort and shelter to passing wildlife.

Each tree sings a song—a result of its surroundings and the depths of its roots.

Trees have all been created for unique and different purposes. And so have you.

May you be a tree that bears much fruit.

CONFUSION

Sometimes, the best thing I can do is take the storm within me, pour it into still waters, and then sit awhile. Here, my thoughts are released from the swirling captivity of my mind, and I find pastures of God's peace.

We demolish arguments and every pretension that sets itself up against the knowledge of God, and we take captive every thought to make it obedient to Christ.

2 Corinthians 10:3-5 NIV

CONFUSION

Five times I've birthed new life. Each time, I've reached a bleak point where doubts warred in my head, and the pain shouted even louder.

When the way gets dark and the lies seem true, one must reach for the Sword and hang onto it tight.

The truth is louder than the lie if you speak it while proclaiming the promise over the feelings.

New life is birthed when fears are conquered.

BEAUTY MAKER

This day, this hour, this moment—
It's all I have right now
To do what's in front of me,
But I fear I don't have the power.

"Don't fear," You say,
"I know you are weak—
My saving arms, with infinite love,
Are here to guide your feet."

"I know you don't have answers;
I know that you're confused.
But here I AM, alive and strong,
With arms to help you through."

"Don't be afraid; don't be perplexed.
Rest in Me instead.
Discover what it truly means
To rest your pretty little head."

"The work is much,
(But the labour sweet).
I'm breathing new life,
Making a way through seas."

Take heart, look up—
Raise your hands to the sky.
Creation still sings
And so will I.

CONFUSION

Losing a rose to eternity is bittersweet—the bitterness of grief is hard to bear, but the hope of heaven yields an everlasting sweetness.

If any of you lacks wisdom, you should ask God, who gives generously to all without finding fault, and it will be given to you.

James 1:5 NIV

CONFUSION

We are sojourners in a foreign land— citizens of heaven—breathing here briefly, with seeds in our hands.

Wisdom is knowing which laws of the land to abide by, which ones to resist, and which ones to shape with our prayers.

All so that our edicts can be carried over barricaded borders and grow beauty again.

BEAUTY MAKER

For so long, it sat there,
barren and fruitless;
The ground beneath me,
haunted by uselessness.

Until Someone so kind,
so loving, so true,
knelt in that dry patch
and knew exactly what to do.

He saw potential,
and began breaking through the fallow.
He invited me to join Him,
with sweat dripping from His brow.

We knelt down together,
and He handed me some seeds.
He looked me in the eye and asked,
"Can you plant these for me, please?"

I did as He said,
buried each seed in.
And then I stepped back,
and watched the real work begin.

I watched as His blood
sprinkled over them all,
and behold, what happened
was a miracle I saw.

Those seeds, by His grace
are growing, one by one.
The beauty keeps on coming,
life given by the Son.

CONFUSION

Are you and I following manmade rebellion, or are our feet treading upon the ancient path fashioned by the Father? The Way where you will find rest for your souls?

Now faith is confidence in what we hope for and assurance about what we do not see.

Hebrews 11:1 NIV

CONFUSION

I often forget to seek wisdom from above,
the wisdom that sees all that is unseen
and has the answers to all I seek.

What does this child need?
Grace, teaching—or just listening?

What does my mind need?
Work, rest, or play?

What does my body need?
Movement, nourishment, or medicine?

What does this friendship need?
Time, investment, or prayer?

Every day, I need wisdom to get through,
but I must embrace wisdom from above.

BEAUTY MAKER

You can't have a garden wild with flowers without getting a little dirt under your nails.

Grit.

CONFUSION

I pedalled my way to the beach
for the day's last light,
to tuck in the ocean
and wish her good night.

As I neared toward her evening song,
the trees told me stories,
and I gladly listened.
The ocean had a lot to say, too,
and my heart tumbled back questions.

Not for the ocean to answer,
no, she is not her Creator.
My brave questions
were for the One who made her—
the One who can sleep through her storms,
the One who can calm her waves in a moment.

BEAUTY MAKER

To search the skies and hills and valleys for 'truth,' only to arrive at an opinion and a deeper dive 'within'—is that a worthy quest?

Our hearts are sure to lead us down paths forged by feelings and filled with boulders of uncertainty.

If we are truly hungry for Truth, He wants to be found. But we must stop looking in the mirror and ask Him to 'open our eyes.'

It's here grace finds us, and our eyes, though still in the land of seeing but never perceiving, begin to discover something quite beyond it.

But the wisdom that comes from heaven is first of all pure; then peace-loving, considerate, submissive, full of mercy and good fruit, impartial and sincere. Peacemakers who sow in peace reap a harvest of righteousness.

James 3:17-18 NIV

BEAUTY MAKER

If everything goes south, can I still find the gifts? If the road is smooth, will I notice the beauty? If the road is dreary, can I unwrap the hidden treasure? And if the road ends, can I find thanks there too?

Can I cover my pilgrimage in prayer, on every step and every turn, on every bend and in every valley?

I know this is what is asked of me—to give thanks in all things. I have the living God in me, showing me how.

Giving thanks in all things is the seed of joy, the precursor to life—abundant life—and opens the door to intimacy with my Creator.

CONFUSION

When you know that you know that you know you're meant to do something—and you receive confirmation after confirmation, followed by revelation after revelation, you know you're on the right track. Even if it doesn't make sense, and you don't know how, you know—He will make a way.

BEAUTY MAKER

The call arrived while I dreamt. I saw the words and felt them too. The sun rose with my pen, and then, right on time, the message arrived. They offered an open door to surrender the old and welcome the new.

My hands got busy praying. I stood fiercely with you in Spirit but it wasn't by sight. We waged war in the heavens, taking captive every thought. Your tears were your offering, and Jesus held them all.

Unity matters. For although we may not agree on everything, we need each other desperately. By only looking at who is right, we miss all the beauty. We win by fighting together, kneeling side-by-side.

CONFUSION

Ancient stories drawn on stone echo loudly within the room— no longer a safety, now an empty cocoon. I cannot stay here, in my old cave of thoughts, drawn in darkness.

The light beckons, my body feels the beat, the sky speaks of colour. The cave is defeated. I've found true freedom beyond the stone walls; my feet now can dance with the stars as my floor. The world I now live in cannot be walled-in—the boundless sky beckons me forth.

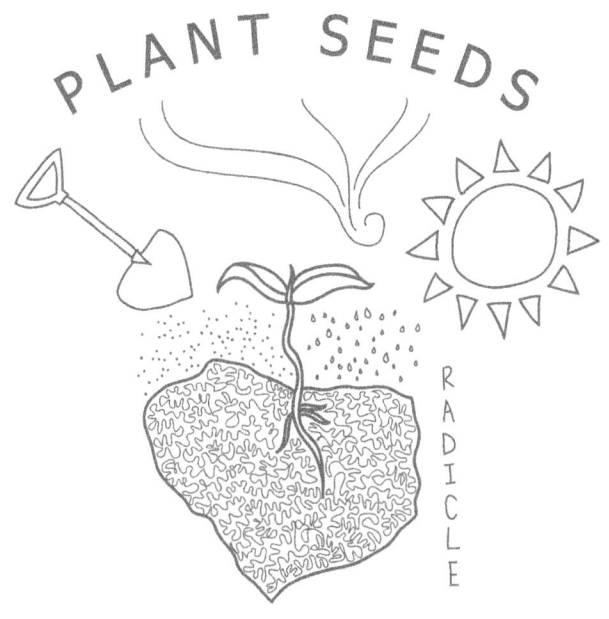

SURRENDER

THE SEED OF FAITH IS PLANTED, THE SOWING OF
RIGHTEOUSNESS BEGINS, AND A HARVEST OF
SOULS IS PREPARED

BEAUTY MAKER

A humble plot of land,
given as a gift.
Dirt mixed with grace,
hidden underneath.

The joy is in the digging;
the faith is in the seed.
The water is in the worship;
the growth is happening.

It's not the work of weather;
it's not the work of wind.
It's the work of the Creator,
and His gracious, loving hand.

The garden is vast and sprawling;
our hands are weak and small.
But, still, His breath is coming
to bring beauty to it all.

So I'll keep on sowing,
and I know you will, too.
Then, we will witness the miracle
that comes from knowing Truth.

SURRENDER

Surrendering to God is not a passive state of helplessness but a deep conviction that there is a greater plan. What can be found here is deep rest, despite the raging seas, and a strength to move past one's natural abilities and into the Promised Land.

It is possible to be in this state of heart, feeling utterly weak and completely broken but also strangely awake to the reality that heaven is near, overflowing with an out-of-this-earth peace.

It's here that grace is found.

BEAUTY MAKER

Perhaps peace is lost
because hands still
grip to control?

Let go.
Palms open.
Bury your seed.

Prayer remedies
minds at war.

You're not in control.

SURRENDER

Look at them. They are young. They are looking for truth, looking for love, and they're looking to you to show them.

Look at them. See their fears; see their joy. See them discover the world around them. They need your guidance.

Look at them. The way Jesus sees them. The way He sees you. They are not a burden. And when culture says so, don't believe it. Being a mother is the most extraordinary opportunity to burn for Him and be a living sacrifice, even when it hurts.

Look at Jesus because He is looking at your children. Let Him carry you, let Him carry all the weight you feel, and then let Him fill you so you can water your little seeds in the garden of motherhood.

BEAUTY MAKER

I thought I was defenceless,
But You declared
Your goodness remains.

I thought I was defenceless,
But there You stood
And called me by name.

I thought I was defenceless,
But You broke through
And covered all my shame.

Now I see Your face,
Eyes filled with love,
Taking away my pain.

You pour out Your grace
And defend me
Over and over again.

SURRENDER

Count your blessings, but hold them loosely. Surrender replaces fear with flowers. It guards your heart with trust that every loss is a brand new beginning for something even better.

Lose the white knuckles.

BEAUTY MAKER

I dare not clench these hands tight, even out of innocent protection of the warmth within them, for each time I try, it flickers dim.

And when the wind blows, and the air mocks with its darkness, all I want to do is hold on harder.

No, these hands must stay open. Surrendered and anointed with the oil of faith—for empty hands release the brightest Light.

They must stay open.

Very truly I tell you, unless a kernel of wheat falls to the ground and dies, it remains only a single seed. But if it dies, it produces many seeds.

John 12:24 NIV

BEAUTY MAKER

I want to follow the narrow path. The way that leads to desert gardens, mountain dancing, valley waterfalls, and meadows of wildflowers—all in adventurous yet trustworthy companionship.

SURRENDER

Rest says I don't have to pave my own way to heaven. Love has already done it for me.

BEAUTY MAKER

I know what's coming now—
the changing of tides,
the desire to surrender,
and Love sustaining me there.

Even when my arms flounder,
those new waves
keep on pushing and rising,
taking me toward a new horizon.

SURRENDER

I want to lay down yesterday's epiphanies for tomorrow's mysteries, replacing current grooves (especially the ones that my heels have slowly dug in) to follow the winds of heaven. If there's more—and I know there is— I want in.

I'll chart my course to the deeper waters.

Those who go out weeping, carrying seed to sow, will return with songs of joy, carrying sheaves with them.

Psalms 126:6 NIV

SURRENDER

I look at my garden and wonder if my seeds or fragile new plants might be eaten by slugs or birds or snails or pulled out by careless little hands—or even forgotten for too long and die from my own neglect. But I do know that if I don't bother planting or trying or learning, only weeds will grow, and so I keep at it—planting seeds and hoping to see the miracle of growth by the sovereign hand of the Beauty Maker.

BEAUTY MAKER

At first I ran and hid,
not wanting to be swallowed up
by the mysterious hand
that wanted to transform me.

But then I wandered and searched
and began to realise,
while others found their uniforms
and gathered in joy for their united cause,
I remained a little different.

I wore the same colour, yes,
but the outfit was not the same.
While I rejoiced with them,
I knew I could not join in.

I was meant to be
a stranger in this world
and chosen
according to the foreknowledge of God
to be transformed
by the mysterious hand of the Spirit.

I was *meant* to be a little different.

And it was then that I stood still,
no longer running,
but surrendered instead.

SURRENDER

When He speaks, mountains move.
When He speaks, seeds bloom.
When He speaks, arrows shoot.
When He speaks, Light breaks through.
When He speaks, His Word proves true.
When He speaks, He fills the room.
When He speaks, heaven falls anew.

Speak, Lord; we are listening to You.

Sow with a view to righteousness [that righteousness, like seed, may germinate]; Reap in accordance with mercy and loving kindness.

Break up your uncultivated ground, For it is time to seek and search diligently for the Lord [and to long for His blessing] Until He comes to rain righteousness and His gift of salvation on you.

Hosea 10:12 AMP

SURRENDER

We leave with the city still sleeping,
heavy mist still hovering
above the mountaintops.

My four loves
tucked into back seat blankets
and one held close against me.

The captain is driving this ship,
and we all know
that the days ahead
will change us in wonderful ways.

There is something about the open road,
something about dreaming under stars,
something about unplanned plans...

I think I'm ready for the journey—
yet again.

BEAUTY MAKER

Her spirit is wonderfully free, her soul fiercely alive, her heart bravely vulnerable, and her faith dangerously hopeful.

When she prays, demons tremble.
When she kneels, mountains shake.
When she loves, souls soften.
When she sings, Truth cuts through.

Her secret:
It's who she knows.

SURRENDER

The days at home with small children can be full and overflowing with physical demands, one after the other.

But despite the constant hum of 'to dos', our children get to see us live (albeit imperfectly) and make a beautiful life, together.

The moments we choose the slow beat of our children's attention, surrendering the need to rush to the never-ending cry of the home (even just for a short while), are the moments that will mark our souls forever. They will mark theirs forever, too.

Stop and smell the roses once in awhile.

BEAUTY MAKER

What if the falling becomes your calling? What if sacrifice is what fills your empty cup? What if the real reward is found in giving?

What if an abundant life isn't found in a bucket list but a life laid down for one beyond your own?

What if your passions come to life within the boundaries of a life poured out for another?

What if we need to rewire our hearts to the idea of a radical life by radically giving it away to Another?

What if receiving looks like serving in all the small moments that never get accolades but leave a legacy of love along the way? What if 'getting rid of what doesn't serve' is a trap, but freedom is found in the pouring out of everything we have for a purpose greater than ourselves?

What if, to find a life filled with extravagant beauty, we must follow the One who gave His for us?

SURRENDER

Offering up your meagre loaves and fishes in mustard seed faith, precedes the miracle of multiplication. Heaven's feast.

*The light shines in the darkness, but
the darkness has not understood it.*

John 1:5 NIV

SURRENDER

Praise paves the way for breakthrough.
Giving thanks precedes the miracle.
Glory-songs revive faith.
Singing truth swings the sword.

Worship is warfare.

BEAUTY MAKER

I released the contents
of my earthen vessel,
entering the void of 'what now?'
with nothing but an empty cup.

It was only then that the clouds,
paths, and immovable mountains
began opening up, filling
my void with a mighty rush.

Heavenly gifts,
with all their mystery,
fragrance, and beauty—

Ready to be discovered.

SURRENDER

I've caught a glimpse of His goodness; I've seen a glimmer of His face. I've watched Him move, and I've heard Him speak.

And I know, from the tips of my outstretched fingers to the heels of my travelling-to-the-mountain-top feet, that there is so much more coming. But first, our whole hearts must wholeheartedly desire Him.

BEAUTY MAKER

Dreams—they make my feet dance and point my toes in the right direction. But they also need time to rest on Heaven's pillow, the room to change, to grow, and to be given vibrant steps for tomorrow.

SURRENDER

It often felt more than I could bare.
But I held on and kept the faith
despite the little strength I had.
What was being birthed in me
was worth it all.

I had said, "Here I am Lord; send me."
And so Love led me here—
to the alter of my temporary comforts
towards the dawn of life.
Something I couldn't even see
or comprehend was taking place
within me.

All I knew was that my obedience
to the path unknown—
the one narrow but free
where I am found weak but strong,
poor but rich,
lowly but loved,
was opening the door
to the Kingdom of Heaven.

So, I planted my seed
and watched it grow.

Search me, God, and know my heart; test me and know my anxious thoughts. See if there is any offensive way in me, and lead me in the way everlasting.

Psalms 139:23-24 NIV

SURRENDER

He's not finished yet.

There are still more
pages to your story.

One day, you'll see that
all these messy yieldings
were actually seeds
destined to adorn
eternity's garden.

Stay the course—
there is more.

BEAUTY MAKER

What is better? To empty my mind of its contents completely, creating space for darkness to fill it? Or to sit in surrender, acknowledge my hunger, and feast on the sweet Word of heaven, letting its goodness nourish my bones as I rest?

Perhaps the very key to meditation is to *fill* my soul with heaven's honey—not empty it for the darkness to find a new home in.

SURRENDER

Home is where—
Good habits are formed.
Celebrations are held.
Stories are shared.
Questions are asked.
Grace is given (again).
Tummies are filled.
Love lives.

Before you know it—
Growing happens.
Gardens are established.
Habits are remembered.
Hospitality brings forth friendships.
And everything is done, together.

Make a home, and give these gifts to your children. But mostly, lead them Home into the hands of the One who carries it all, if we let Him. This is where we can admit that we can't actually do it all perfectly, and our weary bones get the breath they need to keep living, loving, and learning each day, together.

Now he who supplies seed to the sower and bread for food will also supply and increase your store of seed and will enlarge the harvest of your righteousness.

You will be enriched in every way so that you can be generous on every occasion, and through us your generosity will result in thanksgiving to God.

2 Corinthians 9:10-11 NIV

SURRENDER

It starts with a clear mind.
To get there,
you must take a few steps back,
open your eyes,
and pay attention.

The Voice is soft, at first,
and often sounds like thoughts
drifting off into your wild imagination.

But often, it's not.
This is the sound of heaven,
drifting you closer to Love.

Make it pass through the lens of Truth,
and if it comes through
still shimmering with hope,
the only thing left to do
is to surrender to its holy breath.

Take the risk.
Yes, the road might seem a little radical.
Yes, you might look a little fanatical.

But this is not much of a wrestle.
Because what other choice is there
when you love the Voice that spoke,
with all your heart, soul, and mind?

Surrender to the sound of heaven,
Love will meet you at every step.

BEAUTY MAKER

I'm learning—
always learning.
And then relearning.

A beautiful life is filled with surrender.

SURRENDER

When you step out of your safe space into the wild but protected fields of His purpose, remember this: you do not need to be qualified to be obedient, but you do need to be obedient to qualify.

Fruit follows obedience.

BEAUTY MAKER

You have a job that only you can do.
Let Him write it on your heart.

How foolish! What you sow does not come to life unless it dies. When you sow, you do not plant the body that will be, but just a seed, perhaps of wheat or of something else. But God gives it a body as he has determined, and to each kind of seed he gives its own body.

1 Corinthians 15:36-38 NIV

BEAUTY MAKER

I did away with busy for a small moment to simply be, like Mary—to sit with my little loves beside my french lavender and its first debut, to hear the blue wrens singing above and keeping the flower seedlings company.

We read of brave adventures and worlds beyond our own.

I planted seeds in the gardens of little minds in hopeful anticipation of a beautiful harvest.

SURRENDER

It started with a question:
"Please let me see?"

Eyes widen a little more;
lips sing with new soul,
asking Truth to be the anchor
and breathe through humble poems.

Thus begins a new season
and the sound of new song.
Or are they new seeds
given freely to sow?

But he said to me, "My grace is sufficient for you, for my power is made perfect in weakness." Therefore I will boast all the more gladly about my weaknesses, so that Christ's power may rest on me.

2 Corinthians 12:9 NIV

SURRENDER

Do away with striving.
Let your pulse slow,
And your heart quicken,
As you let the silence in His presence
Overtake you as you listen.

Let the peaceful moment find you,
Breathing deep,
Breathing slow,
As you let your shoulders drop
And all of your burdens go.

The only way to receive
and unravel
His beautiful grace,
Is to give Him all your heart
And gaze into His face.

BEAUTY MAKER

My Father in heaven,

I see my faults. I see my sin. I see how I fail to live up to Your standard of perfection. It grieves me and tries to withhold the potential of all You want to do in and through me. This is why I am surrendering to You now.

The only way to conquer this darkness is by laying it down in light of the death and resurrection of Your Son, Jesus, and bringing it to the cross in repentance. Only here can I know that Your grace has covered the cost so I do not have to spend my whole life trying to pay for it.

Death has lost its power over me. Instead, Life has found me here, on my knees in sorrow for what I have done, and I receive the strength to walk forward in Your grace and love for all eternity.

In fact, Your grace, mercy and loving kindness has brought me here to repent. Even this humble act I cannot claim as my own.

You chose me to be Yours, to be purified here, and to offer my life to You in worship as a response to Your Great Beauty.

I am Yours.
May Your will be done in me.

Amen.

SURRENDER

It was only then,
when I held in hand
each option—
each and every one,
with an open mind,
a yielded spirit,
willing also,
to own its ripples,
even towards the option
my heart was reluctant to,
that I knew whichever
God prompted me to do,
for His many reasons,
that He would also provide
the grace to face
whatever it held.

It was only then
that the peace came,
and I heard Him speak.

BEAUTY MAKER

Glitter turns back to dust if there is
no Truth within it.

SURRENDER

Every day awakens,
like an empty page to write,
and every day, I'm at the threshold,
awakening a new line of sight.

My feet are on the threshing floor,
harvesting my thoughts,
expecting to re-emerge
with a concept firmly caught.

The dawn of every day
brings new opportunities,
but my hands remain present
to each day's humble needs.

I'm not the same as yesterday,
(I don't expect to be),
and I know that crossing this threshold
will help blind eyes to see.

So, while I'm deep in threshing
the wheat from the husks,
I'll live each day knowing,
In His timing I can trust.

But he continues to pour out more and more grace upon us. For it says, "God resists you when you are proud but continually pours out grace when you are humble."

James (Jacob) 4:6 TPT

SURRENDER

Gifts are given to fly—soaring highest when surrendered back to where they came.

BEAUTY MAKER

There is something to be said about journeying honestly through one's thought-garden, bringing clippers in one hand, seeds in the other, a shovel in the pocket, eyes to behold new colours, arms eager to plant, and knees ready to kiss the earth.

SURRENDER

Those shoes that have carried you—that have stomped through mud, hurdled over lies, trekked under stars, and helped gather blooms for your heart—it's time to pass those pilgrim stories on to other weary feet to find support within them, too.

There are new shoes to wear-in, more stories to tell, more blooms to hold, and more stars to behold.

New shoes, while not always comfy and bringing blisters (for a while), are still the right shoes for you, for right now.

You are stepping out onto an adventurous new path of good works—one that has been prepared in advance, especially for you.

BEAUTY

BEARING FRUIT IN THE LIGHT OF GRACE—
THIS IS WHERE THE GLORY OF THE LORD RISES UPON YOU

BEAUTY MAKER

A new day
with new light,
a sunny bloom
sprung up in the night.

The tree bloomed purple,
the wrens flew in.
The long, dark nights
always have an end.

Dawn emerged—
bright, faithful, and true.
A promise fulfilled—
a gift once cocooned.

The song she sang
when all was still dark
has awakened the dawn
and put gold in her heart.

Her petals, like the sun,
her fragrance made sweet.
Her song now a light
for eyes that can see.

Now she stands
as one with the Son;
for it's there her strength lies
and all that's to come—

For as the soil makes the sprout come up and a garden causes seeds to grow, so the Sovereign Lord will make righteousness and praise spring up before all nations.

Isaiah 61:11 NIV

BEAUTY MAKER

I am not complaining,
although sometimes I do.
Why must my limitations persecute me?
I willingly and joyfully
accepted this invitation,
fully knowing.

The aching of it all is teaching me,
training me,
to fix my eyes on the unseen,
the not-here-yet,
the beauty of what is to come.

All of my doing
and achieving
and working
must stand still.

And so I find myself
learning a new skill—
the act of receiving
while my weary legs rest.

I pick up the vibrant threads of grace
and allow myself to weave its beauty
one stitch at a time,
unraveling the silken red,
staring closely,
squinting from afar,
and beholding
the picture that is unfolding.

God knows—
I can do nothing,
but let my empty hands
receive the beauty,
and I can do nothing else
but try and tell of it.

BEAUTY

All I knew when I started working in my garden was that I desired beauty in my own backyard.

I wanted fragrant flowers climbing up my fence in spring, daisies to smile at me daily, lavender to remind me of a book I once wrote, and enough blooms to fill a vase here and there, so the beauty could follow me inside and sing on the dining room table.

I did not realise, when I bundled up those seedlings and drove them home, that I had just enrolled in the school of gardening, majoring in life.

I readied the soil and broke up the fallow ground while wrestling with ideas and thoughts and the worries of the world. I buried the seedlings and placed them into the ground, as I surrendered my own ideas and put my trust in the Master Gardener.

And the beauty? It's arriving over and over again, proving the Word to be true. Now the first fruits can sing on my table, blessing those who gather around it.

I'm learning, always learning, and then relearning—a beautiful life is full of surrender.

BEAUTY MAKER

There was a point when I realised, as a mother, that if I wanted to enjoy life, I was responsible for bringing goodness into my days. No one else was going to do it for me. Now I know:
I surrender as each new sun rises, and ask God to come and show me how to subdue and rule the day's troubles, for the sake of my whole family.

I must repent of my victim mentality and allow the light of God's grace to redeem me even on the most difficult of days.

There are no perfect days. There are always runny noses and crying babies and disagreeing children and sleepless nights and mess and hungry tummies.

I'm learning, though, even as I write, the importance of stewarding wonder and beauty in the light of grace, by looking to the One who created each day and, with unveiled eyes, choosing to rejoice and be glad in it, despite what it may bring.

There is a grace that saves, and there is a grace that sustains. I need the latter. May I take hold of it today.

BEAUTY

How easy is it to see the beauty in extravagance—the mansion, the expensive attire, the endless blooming garden?

How unusual is it to find beauty in the absence of extravagance—the cosy home, the simple attire, the single rose in a small garden?

How sad is it when luxury leaves a void of loneliness, anxiety, and despair?

How beautiful is it when an extravagant life is given up to fulfill the will of God?

Heaven sees the one and only precious coin worth more than all the rest.

I would rather have unveiled eyes than an extravagant life and experience extravagant Love more than anything else.

The riches found in seeking the Kingdom are not of this world.

BEAUTY MAKER

I want to *see* Glory—His beauty redeeming everything. And in those moments of pure, surrendered vision, I will plant seeds of joy by whispering, "Thank you." Isn't that the secret to a shining life?

I don't mean just painting rainbows in the dirt; I mean getting on my knees—even in those dark night trenches—and planting a wildly colourful, fragrant garden, seed by seed, thanks by thanks (even in the not-enoughs and lack of triumphs), and then lying in it with eyes staring deep into the harvest moon, surrounded by a chorus of stars, harvesting a thank-full heart, high on heaven's Glory. I was made for a life like this.

I want to see God's glory. In everything. Oh, I want to truly see—beauty in everything.

BEAUTY

To have a flourishing home...

I am not sure the work will ever be done, but I get glimpses of the beauty every so often as I step back and see the unseen.

It's slowly unraveling like a garden, seed by seed, water drop by water drop, prayer by prayer.

I keep asking God to take what we have in all of its limitations and to lift it beyond the natural and into the realm of His abundance.

For it is by grace you have been saved, through faith—and this is not from yourselves, it is the gift of God—not by works, so that no one can boast.

For we are God's handiwork, created in Christ Jesus to do good works, which God prepared in advance for us to do.

Ephesians 2:8-10 NIV

BEAUTY

No one sees the world
how *you* see it.
Please, tell me the beauty
that your eyes see,
that I may see the miracles too.

There is a shimmer in your eyes
that traces the stars
into patterns I can't see,
discovers miracles
that are hidden to me,
and digs up opals
that sing of amazement.

Please, lend me your eyes.
Tell me of the beauty *you* see.

BEAUTY MAKER

There comes a point
when the enlarging
is no longer hidden.
It is now undeniably visible.

What life is she creating?

What started as a tiny seed,
invisible from the human eye
is about to take over her life.
It is the 'pearl of great price.'

What beauty is she birthing?

In one realm,
the weight of it is heavy,
and in another,
it is light.

What treasure is she storing?

There will come a time when
those dreams, whispers, nudges
will walk around
with lives of their own.

And she,
a vessel made from clay,
forever moulded by Love,
pours her whole life out, again.

BEAUTY

I'm changing and growing and creating and testing and wanting my space to be a colourful eclectic tapestry of foraged treasures but also structured and ordered and then humble and practical but then sometimes lavishly extravagant. Then I clean everything out to be quietly meditative but dream of lively chatter too.

I'll always be found in the wonder of the gloriously never-ending recreating of all the possibilities of beauty and the impossibility of finding them all at once—

Perpetually in pursuit of the unfathomable.

BEAUTY MAKER

We will never know just how many stars actually fly unless we take the time to be captivated by the miracle of the ones glued there for a while.

Enjoying the shimmer of many small wonders helps keep the darkness alight with hope.

I am the true vine, and my Father is the gardener. Remain in me, as I also remain in you. No branch can bear fruit by itself; it must remain in the vine. Neither can you bear fruit unless you remain in me.

John 15:1, 4 NIV

BEAUTY MAKER

Family holds a beautiful glimpse into the kingdom of heaven. God designed families, and He longs to see them restored and redeemed. Being part of a family gives you the choice to give up your life to serve, love and encourage.

But I am not just talking about our immediate families but also the extended family of God—our brothers and sisters in Christ. This also means looking upon those who have not yet found a home within God's family as precious ones whom God loves and longs to be brought into His family. If God desires flourishing families, then He especially longs to pour out His love and grace toward families that are strained or fractured or struggling.

I believe families hold a beautiful key to bringing the kingdom of heaven to earth.

May we unite together and press on towards the goal of loving our Father so extravagantly that we also devote our lives to care and tend to His family.

BEAUTY

Maybe it's not *what* you have
but the stories they tell.

Maybe it's not *what* you achieve
but the legacy you'll leave.

BEAUTY MAKER

Harvest moon,
large it looms,
sowing the seeds,
while dancing on hills.

Singing my song,
shouting my thanks,
deep breaths and eyes gazing,
fixed on God's face.

One thing I ask from the Lord, this only do I seek: that I may dwell in the house of the Lord all the days of my life, to gaze on the beauty of the Lord and to seek him in his temple.

Psalms 27:4 NIV

BEAUTY MAKER

The only difference between an ordinary moment and a holy moment is a torn veil and the bare feet of reverence.

BEAUTY

I cast my desperate breath and fished for more strength, and it came back still, with nothing left. But the wind, with all its mystery, swirled and swayed and filled my small basket, again and again.

The unpredictable nature of life's waves prove unstable, and my finite hands easily exhaust the meagre contents of strength found within them. All I can say is the infinite goodness of God is surely good because, despite it all, the beauty of His love keeps finding me, again and again, and that's the glorious miracle of all.

His grace is sufficient.

BEAUTY MAKER

I feel totally unqualified but also deeply called and also completely certain that's how God likes to reveal His golden fingerprints of glory through our lives.

Here I am, Lord. Send me.

BEAUTY

Emotions do not rule my heart.
I may feel them...
But trust them? I can't.

I should acknowledge them,
sometimes make them tea,
or simply ask them to leave,
while knowing the Keeper of my heart
can transform all that tastes bitter
and give sweet remedy.

I can not always trust my heart
or consistently follow its lead
because it's often clouded
with things like weariness or anxiety.

So when my heart and flesh fail,
and the hot, dry winds gale,
I won't sit in guilt,
or wallow or wilt,
or even decide on a whim.

I'll guard my heart
so flowers might grow.
And beauty can flow
out from within.

BEAUTY MAKER

It can lie dormant for months and months, waiting underground. And then, after a small, brief soaking, burst into bloom again.

The optimism of a crocus.

The desert and the parched land will be glad; the wilderness will rejoice and blossom. Like the crocus, it will burst into bloom; it will rejoice greatly and shout for joy.

Isaiah 35:1-2 NIV

BEAUTY MAKER

I want to turn every note
around me into a song.
A sound graced with heaven's fragrance
that invites others to sway.

A song that arrives as a gift
because of the One who lives in me—
who opened the eyes of my eyes,
so that I could really see.

Melodies laced with the beat of Truth
to find a Life that is rich
on Love's narrow Way.

I want to learn this song forever,
and sway.

BEAUTY

I'm swimming in grace—
oceans of it.

Finally, believers, whatever is true, whatever is honourable and worthy of respect, whatever is right and confirmed by God's word, whatever is pure and wholesome, whatever is lovely and brings peace, whatever is admirable and of good repute; if there is any excellence, if there is anything worthy of praise, think continually on these things [centre your mind on them, and implant them in your heart].

Philippians 4:8 AMP

BEAUTY

Morning hugs, teas in the sun,
finding time for some one-on-one

Reading true words, prayers as I learn,
resting on Sundays is where I return

Kiss before work, words kindly put,
making small efforts in how I look

A moment to read, new words penned,
living inspired with new thoughts in my head

Meeting together, sharing with one another,
praying for wisdom for each other

Slowly forming faithful habits,
that are big enough to change what happens

Anchoring a busy life while keeping in sight,
what matters most, in eternity's light

BEAUTY MAKER

Experience is a heavenly language. We all long for experiences in this life that will somehow transcend time. And they all do. Every experience touches our soul in some way. Which is why finding 'closure' for a life lost is actually impossible. Encountering the life of another eternal soul will forever leave an imprint deep within ours.

We are all searching for signs and wonders that tell us that there is more to life than what we see with our eyes, and we are looking to truly experience the wonder of a perfect love that cannot be found within the limitations of humanity.

We all need experiences that cut through the boundaries of time and space and stamp a promise in our soul's passport for an eternity of the most beautiful experience we will ever embark on.

I've had a short lifetime of these moments. Coincidences too serendipitous to even be called coincidental and hindsight's wisdom to see the hand of God in it all.

All because I once knelt in surrender. All because I was hungry just to truly know and love the Creator of the universe, and because of it, time itself, nor anything in this life or even the ending of it, cannot take the grace I received away.

These experiences are deeply embedded within my soul for all of eternity. They say, "There is a God. And He loves me."

But I also know that to experience this kind of divine beauty, I must be willing to wander through the desert for a while as a sojourner who knows this world is not her home.

BEAUTY

Take note of who arrives on your path (you need not seek the crowds). The heart that arrives in peace is ready for the seed, if your hands are willing and ready to serve.

BEAUTY MAKER

My limitations, when given to the overflowing supply of God's limitlessness, become the fuel to power His grace in my life, revolutionising my lack into more than enough.

BEAUTY

It was just an ordinary moment
but also not so ordinary at all.
Why the jacaranda tree pulled
at my heart the year before,
I wasn't quite sure.

It was only one year later,
sitting cross-legged on a blanket
under a blooming jacaranda
with Melody's three children,
laughing and playing with mine,
that I learnt why—

Jacaranda means 'fragrant,'
and Melody had one with
branches strong enough
for her kids to spend many years
swinging from and playing under.
It stood tall and on guard
in front of the house she lived in,
before she rose to Heaven's gardens.

Its timely significance
to the release of *Fragrant Melodies*–
the book dedicated to her
with her songs
on the first and last pages
was finally understood.

We now call the purple display
the 'Fragrant Melody' tree,
our eyes open to the intricacies
God designs to display His glory.

Even here, there is beauty.
Even here, out of the ashes—
if you have eyes to see.

BEAUTY MAKER

Grace doesn't always swoop in with the answer we hoped for, but He always gives us hope for the future and perseverance to weather whatever's in store.

BEAUTY

In the cultivation of small, faithful rhythms, we discover the seeds of His wisdom and the barren soil of our souls slowly blossoming.

BEAUTY MAKER

Where is beauty?
Is beauty still hidden
in the humble corners of life
for the eyes that can see?

Where does our desire end,
and where did it begin?
Will it ever be fully satisfied
on this side of heaven?

Can beauty speak?
Can it sing?
Is it *actually* possible to
find it in everything?

I'm getting to know Beauty
as an entity
a divine glory
a mystery
a Person.

I saw a glimpse of Eden
and heard a love song from Beauty
because He let me see Him.

BEAUTY

Yes, Beauty sings!
Once, He brought seven wrens
to my dirty window,
just to chorus over me.

Even through that window,
frosted from sticky little fingers
and tainted with the original sin.

The day after that miracle,
even with my view
clouded with 'to-dos'
and one hundred new messes,
questions, and requests,
before the clock struck 8 a.m.,
my thoughts turned again
to that dirty window.

Another little wren!
Perched on my windowsill
for a few special seconds,
to sing to me again.

I thought they were just
passing through, gifting me
one love note from heaven
to encourage my weary heart.

But they stayed to sing to me
from that day on.

BEAUTY MAKER

Father, would you unveil my eyes
to Your Word all around me?
May it wrap me in love
and sustain me from within
to walk this ordinary day,
beholding the glory of heaven
and finding home in Your hands.

Turn my daily appointments
into divine ones.
Turn my small threads of faithfulness
into a golden tapestry,
and turn the fragility of my humanity
into a fragrant melody.

BEAUTY

Its origin is hidden from the human eye, but it arrives to sustain all life. More than 80% of me is made of it. It has no colour, no scent, and is completely transparent. It holds a certain secrecy that will always be a mystery, and yet, we can't live without it.

The Son has opened the eyes of my heart a bit more widely to see the mystery of water's beauty.

You see, there was once an old religious tradition— one must be purified with water from a living, flowing stream before being able to sit with God. But now, every new day, He washes me clean, making me worthy to commune.

The Son brought with Him Living Water— moving, speaking, breathing, and cleansing. His origin is hidden from the human eye, but He arrived to sustain all life. Everything I am is because of Him. He has no colour, no scent, and He's completely transparent. He holds a certain secrecy that will always be a mystery, and yet, I can't truly live without Him.

My desire is to engage with this Living Water, petitioning, communing, and living together— forever.

But the fruit of the Spirit [the result of His presence within us] is love [unselfish concern for others], joy, [inner] peace, patience [not the ability to wait, but how we act while waiting], kindness, goodness, faithfulness, gentleness, self-control. Against such things there is no law.

Galatians 5:22-23 AMP

Thus, by their fruit you will recognize them.

Matthew 7:20 NIV

BEAUTY

My heart always told me that creating needed to be part of my every day. But I've never known precisely how it should be embodied and often wondered about its purpose if it even has one.

I have found myself instinctively following sign posts that would lead to colourful making stations, each with new materials to play with. I would say that my hands do the forming, but I'm learning that the process actually works a spiritual formation in me. And when the clock tells me I'm done, I leave with an extra patchwork for my life-quilt and another story to sing.

I don't always see the purpose of creating when my hands are deep in the work, but I'm learning there always is one.

My eyes are ever-widening to the truth that we all bear the image of the creative Creator and that to make art with our very lives reveals a glorious dimension of His heart. And there's certainly a beautiful purpose in that.

BEAUTY MAKER

What are you afraid of? That the call on your life is too grand? That it's too humble?

The truth is, it's both.

God uses ordinary clay jars to pour His treasure into.

This is the grace outpouring.

BEAUTY

Don't forget the humble work of giving your time, energy, and love for 'one.' It is not a waste of time.

Raising your child, meeting that friend, serving that stranger—it's the small, humble gestures given in the name of Love that make the call on your life beautifully significant.

Those who are faithful in the small will be given more, and to whom much is given, much is required. Kingdom principles are the foundation of a shimmering life.

BEAUTY MAKER

I used to believe I could only be beautiful if I forced myself into a straight enough line and ordered my thoughts, actions, and attitudes into an aesthetically pleasing perfect package.

But every day, I am dismayed at the disarray I find myself in.

I haven't given up on the process because every day, I'm choosing to grow in the right direction, but I've discovered the key to making beauty in the midst of my inevitable failures and flaws.

Grace.

Let us not become weary in doing good, for at the proper time we will reap a harvest if we do not give up.

Galatians 6:9 NIV

BEAUTY MAKER

To be awakened to Beauty
is to need it
and to need it
is to ask for it
and to ask for it
is to see it
and to see it
is to live it
and to live it
is to become it.

BEAUTY

God's creation communicates.

BEAUTY MAKER

Trees of righteousness reach with longing toward heaven's glory. But the way up is down. We must root ourselves in the Truth, accept His grace, and grow, g r O W, G R O W.

He who supplies the seed will surely reap the harvest.

BEAUTY

Motherhood provides a daily choice to follow Jesus in a thousand small ways that make me more like Him.

It's here I set myself apart from society's pace and drawn into a space where I cultivate belonging, safety, beauty, growth, and a place where flaws are seen—often—but never result in rejection. Within these four walls, we do not expect nor offer perfection, but grace covers a multitude of mistakes.

Within these four walls, souls are shaped for eternity. Therefore, I will step aside from the cares of the outside and retain steadfast focus on the lives within.

BEAUTY MAKER

I almost missed the rain when it finally came. If I wasn't listening, I wouldn't have seen it. But its grace fell gently and slowly, and purple flowers now carpet the ground where I was planted.

There, I sang, now kneeling in the purple shade of a tree that was once a tiny mustard seed in me.

And what I expected to be the chorus was, in fact, just a magical prelude.

BEAUTY

I once abandoned my soul's hunger to create for a long, long time.

Who has time to make life beautiful when it takes all your might just to put one foot in front of the other? My journal gathered dust, the paintbrushes were left to rust, and the garden within me begged the overgrown weeds to simply wither and die.

I realise now by learning the hard way, that letting my hands find joy in creating throughout my own ordinary, hidden days tends to my soul's garden and keeps it watered and filled with colour.

Thankfully, the Master Gardener came to remind me of this truth—that He created me to bring richness and colour in the place where He planted me.

I was made to create in the humble rhythms of life while providing an invitation to commune with the Great Artist Himself (especially in all the hidden ways), which is actually the point of it all, I think.

BEAUTY MAKER

When my weariness grows too much to bear, I will promptly and forcefully sit myself at the table of this day, discover its delicious wonder and wholesome beauty, and rediscover the presence of God in it all. I'll find joy in the enjoyment of it and let it blow the dreary fog right out of me.

The heavens declare the glory of God; the skies proclaim the work of his hands. Day after day they pour forth speech; night after night they reveal knowledge.

They have no speech, they use no words; no sound is heard from them. Yet their voice goes out into all the earth, their words to the ends of the world.

Psalms 19:1-4 NIV

BEAUTY MAKER

I tried to reach You. My branches stretched high toward the stars while my leaves grew buds, anticipating the bloom, longing for the spring.

I couldn't make my way to those acres of time we once shared, just You and I. But my roots anchored me and, without any other option, grew deeply—deeper and deeper. And my trunk grew strong—stronger and stronger. And then it opened up and housed things, became a shelter for others, and I took comfort in the company.

I know You heard my call for help because help came. You sent the birds with extravagant love notes tied to their wings.

Those rainbow lorikeets and their loud promise of grace. The prettiest blue wren and his friends with their reminder of your mercy— every single morning. The willy wagtails and their steadfast joy for life.

I tried to reach You, but You sent help instead. You rescued me again.

BEAUTY

Two empty cups of tea;
your fragrance left its memory.
You brought your heavenly offering
and showed me your heartfelt poetry.
What captured me was what I could see—
your obedience and vulnerability.

You thanked me for swimming ahead,
but I have you to thank instead.
Your melodies, sung from the depths,
will reach hearts, prepared in advance.
I'm cheering you on, my kindred friend.
May God bless what's in your hand.

Arise, shine, for your light has come, and the glory of the Lord rises upon you.

Isaiah 60:1 NIV

BEAUTY

I've never been more awake to the seasons than I am right now. Could it be that, for the first time in my life, I've planted my own garden and watched it as it slept and then witnessed it awaken at the time it was designed to?

Or could it be that, at every solemn street corner, the story that's told is that life right now is a never-ending winter?

Seasons bring hope, and each one its own unique sweetness. When spring skips in with its daisy-covered hat, there is someone sitting across the globe, readying to hide away from the cold. We all don't experience the same season at the same time.

I think God created seasons to remind us of this and also that there will always be the turning over from one cold winter to another colourful spring. One only needs time.

BEAUTY MAKER

It's grace
that saved me
from that cowering corner.
It's grace
that invited me in.

It's grace
that marked me for
Heaven forever.
It's grace
I'm swimming in.

It's grace
that's refining my heart
in the fire.
It's grace
that lets me see.

It's grace
that draws my hands
to surrender.
It's grace
that sets me free.

It's grace
that redeems my
past and future.
It's grace
that gives me peace.

It's grace
that points the way
to wonder.
It's grace
that reveals beauty.

BEAUTY

Divine glory and beauty—both undefinable, both pointing to the other. Moments caught in the awe and splendour of beauty provide an invitation into a transcendent experience to glimpse God's glory and rest in His beautiful presence.

BEAUTY MAKER

There are times when I write to forge new pathways through my mind. There are times when I have to relinquish the pen to live deeply, and sometimes, writing thereafter becomes the breath that spills out from the overflow.

There are times when I glean gold from the written words of others. There are times when reading is the key that unlocks hidden dreams.

There are times when poems pray what I cannot speak. There are times when I send cries through the skies to land timely in hearts.

And then there are times when words miraculously align for others, planting seeds and sprouting a harvest in eternity's garden.

Words are precious; words are free. Some words can be wild, untamed, and ugly, while others bring conviction, hope, and peace.

Let's use words to make beauty.

BEAUTY

The most artistic display of beauty I've ever experienced is seeing the lengths God goes to touch the very depths of our souls with His love.

BEAUTY MAKER

I clearly remember the moment the wind brought the whisper that God was going to take me into the wilderness and woo my heart to His. I did not expect to be quite literally 'barren' and wandering through the desert of infertility for many years.

Another day brought rain; the words that fell there declared that there was a 'sweet fragrance' to be poured from my life for the benefit of others. That brief soaking was long forgotten but suddenly unearthed just after I was birthing a book 14 years later called *Fragrant Melodies,* which continues to bless more than just a few.

Another day, the tide rolled in with a different word, quite pretty in its stance. It said "light is coming" and "rise with the morning sun."

Our beautiful little 'light bringer,' our fourth child, born at dawn, given the name that was chosen years before: Lucy Grace, arrived soon after.

I could probably fill a whole book on the poetry He has written in my life, and perhaps, one day, I will. Or maybe, even better—one day, I'll meet you with, quite literally, all the time in the world, and we will read together of the glory He has written in the books of our lives, in the light of eternity.

But what I'll tell you now is this—it seems to me that God takes a lot of delight in speaking poetically, but, even more so, creating poetry out of our every days. There's a special rhythm to His words and complex intricacies to their meanings. One thing I know is—I want to dance to their beautiful melody forever and ever.

BEAUTY

Grace has turned my life
upside down and inside out.
My heart and flesh fail,
but my soul is still stamped
'forever loved.'

I'll never be the same
because of what He gave up.
Open the windows;
let the warm breeze blow.

And open your arms to hope.

BLESSING

THE OVERFLOW OF GRACE,
POURED OUT FOR ANOTHER

BEAUTY MAKER

The promise stood firm—
"My grace is sufficient."

I can see the fiery trial.
I can see the limitations.
I can see my humanity—
my weakness,
my struggles
and discomforts.

These trials are no strange things.
I expect them,
rise to them,
but I still do not like them.

I put on the armour.
Stand firm.
Stand firm.
Stand firm.

Darkness is not darkness
with Him here with me.
And then,
despite what I see,
what I feel,
or what is happening,
grace still rains down.

It waters the ground I tread,
and the roses of His glory
burst forth in love
all around me.

BLESSING

In the end,
Beauty always wins.

In the end,
Light breaks forth
and reveals the silhouette
of His promises over me.

Now what is in
these once empty hands?

A basket full of grace—to share.

BEAUTY MAKER

I've been called out—
set apart,
led to the quiet place,
away from the busy heart.

Stillness is the aim;
prayer is the call.
I'm drawing closer and closer
to what I was made for.

To hear the wings of a butterfly,
to watch the clouds roll and sweep,
to be led as time would lead—
meekly petitioning.

The heart of life is in the seed,
beauty encased in every gift.
I am here now to say—
this is my offering.

BLESSING

I am becoming increasingly aware that the things we do in the flesh affect the Spirit, and the things we do in the Spirit, affect the flesh.

Everything is spiritual.

BEAUTY MAKER

Sometimes a prayer closet is needed, but sometimes, we just need to put our prayers in our pockets and bring them wherever we go.

Call to me and I will answer you and tell you great and unsearchable things you do not know.

Jeremiah 33:3 NIV

BEAUTY MAKER

I didn't realise how an ordinary moment, a heap of uncertainty, a sip of courage, and a willing spirit would open the door to new and fragile beginnings.

Clumsily wearing in new shoes that I needed to 'grow into' while treading into the ground of a fresh day with an apron on were really my prayers, offering up the gifted tools in my belt to use for the building of God's house were really my praises, and following the Truth of His Word was really my adoration for all He'd done.

My life turned into the fragrant melody. My life became His poetry.

The works themselves never brought the beauty or the blessing, the encouragement or the help of the Spirit. It was the obedience, done out of a response to love.

Just as each one of you has received a special gift [a spiritual talent, an ability graciously given by God], employ it in serving one another as [is appropriate for] good stewards of God's multi-faceted grace [faithfully using the diverse, varied gifts and abilities granted to Christians by God's unmerited favour].

1 Peter 4:10 AMP

Remember this: Whoever sows sparingly will also reap sparingly, and whoever sows generously will also reap generously.

Each of you should give what you have decided in your heart to give, not reluctantly or under compulsion, for God loves a cheerful giver.

And God is able to bless you abundantly, so that in all things at all times, having all that you need, you will abound in every good work.

2 Corinthians 9:6-8 NIV

BLESSING

God continues turning the tables in my mind upside down to reveal garden beds filled with purple and white and rose-coloured foxgloves.

Why do the small daily habits and the sowing of His Word have such a transforming effect over time?

Why does laying down my whole life for 'the least of these' to serve and encourage and teach in love lead to experiencing blessings in the most peculiar of ways?

Why are the most humble, desperate moments of weakness the most powerful? Why is such wonderful freedom found on the narrow path? Why is it so productive to rest?

These notions seem like mysteries and maybe even complete nonsense to those not wearing the same glasses. Spiritual sight transforms an ordinary table set to dine into a continual feast of communion.

The tables keep turning and transforming into a special kind of uncommon beauty.

This transformation keeps bringing my knees to the dirt to plant my seed. This transformation turns my life into a blooming garden, reflecting the Kingdom of Heaven.

BEAUTY MAKER

It is not fortune nor fame I want.
I just wish to be seen
in life's ups and downs
and in all of the in-betweens.

My heart, heard and known.
Someone to listen with kindness;
someone to lean in, in love,
accepting both words or silence.

It's not a destination I want,
to accomplish the top of the peak.
It's more 'a way of life'
that my heart tells me to seek.

A forever climb, hands entwined,
rest for head and feet,
and my heart, always home in Love—
sweet communion on every street.

I don't want fame nor fortune
or anything big or grand.
My heart seeks something
that cannot be held in my hand.

Invisible from the touch of light
or given by any man.
Just to be *truly* seen and fully known—
and loved for who I am.

Here, I stand.

BLESSING

Why did I go out to pick flowers after the sun had set? I knelt there, casting light over the sea of blooming cosmos, and harvested them, one by one.

They stood there, tall and slender, bright and cheerful. They did not mind the loud rumbles and flashes of light. The frogs chorused all around me, louder and louder by the second.

Here I am, reaping a basket full of blooms from the seeds I planted in winter, all just to smile at my table in spring. For my friends, of course, who will be joining me soon.

I sow, and I pray. I listen, and I wait.

And then the words come. They don't mind the weather, or even if it's night. They come when they come, and I try not to put up too much of a fight.

Why do I do this? Why do I pay attention to the whispers of little details weaving their way in and through everything that I do? I can't help but pick them all up.

Yes, dear friend—I picked them for you.

BEAUTY MAKER

What if God called you to do the most humble, unseen work and that it would cause you to kneel and wrestle and question and dig and till the uncultivated ground of your soul, but it would be done on your knees with Love kneeling right beside you?

What if a lot of the answers you were looking for required nothing but simple childlike faith, that the wisdom found would be contrary to what you thought, and it would require your dreams and desires to be buried in the dirt, your hands to be emptied, and your soul to water it in worship as you planted it all?

What if the promise of a new day keeps arising, and you see that, again and again, when your single seed dies, it has the ability to produce many more, and that the wind will help you carry those seeds over hills and through valleys, uncovering an uncommon beauty, redeeming everything in its time?

What if an abundant, blessed life means living this process over and over but that the fruit will last forever, and the result will be one where your roots grow deep and your branches stretch high, all for the benefit of others and the beautiful glory of heaven?

It's time to plant your seed.

BLESSING

I'm learning what it means to truly live in grace.
Not the grace that comes in, gives you what you
want, and provides material favour.

But the grace that draws you to your knees and
gives you the breath to pray bold prayers like...

Make me small.
Make me empty.
Make me weak.
Make me poor.
Make me gentle.
Make me meek.

So that Your glory, Your power,
and Your beautiful grace
can be poured out from me.

And then feel it rain gently, in power and love,
opening the door for Beauty to be revealed in the
most uncommon ways.

Here, in the ordinary, the mundane, even in the
mess, and even when all I see is drained of colour,
grace comes in, and sends me love note after love
note.

Peace pours over me,
and I drink from its rivers.

This is the grace I'm learning to live in.

BEAUTY MAKER

Communion flies above confusion and suffering, enters with nothing in hand but a vessel for grace to pour from your hands to another's, asking heaven to come down to earth once more.

Here, words are neither a sentiment nor a question but a very real way of communing.

Here, the human heart arises to plead with the Divine while burying personal preferences in order to offer the gift of a new threshold on the shoreline of grace and an invitation to sail to new worlds.

The wonder of a blessing is how it mysteriously bounds back to you as a two-fold gift. This miraculous way of speech is a worthy treasure to unearth.

*It is more blessed to
give than to receive.*

Acts 20:35b NIV

BEAUTY MAKER

A Blessing for the Reader

May you take shelter
in the strong and mighty fortress of the Word.

May it reveal the weeds in your soil
as you cultivate and dig through the Logos faithfully.

May you take heed of its treasure
and find freedom on your knees in repentance.

May your heart be your sacrifice
as you seek God's will for your life.

May the seed of faith within you produce a tangible hope
that you will reap what you sow.

May the harvest of your seed
bear a basket of fruit, filled to overflowing.

May you keep finding grace
in the light of surrender,
and may you take its gifts from the citadel to the streets.

May you be a vessel for the Beauty Maker
to bring heaven's kingdom to earth
to see His beautiful glory.

May you be a Beauty Maker,
and may you find beauty—in surrender.

BLESSING

A Morning Blessing

May you find joy in God's presence as you go about your day,
bringing order and beauty within your home and family.

May you hear Heaven's wisdom as it calls,
taking heed of its advice,
and may God direct your paths
and the decisions that weigh heavily upon your heart.

May God provide abundant patience
and grant you the strength you need
to work with your hands and serve others humbly.

May you live a life of prayer
while passing on the baton
to run this race to win the prize,
of an eternity with Jesus, side by side.

May God help you when you're tempted,
when your thoughts go astray.
May they be brought back with truth
and made captive to His ways.

May you use this day wisely—
building, shaping, creating, and serving, all for God.
But may you do so without striving,
knowing His grace enfolds all you do.

BEAUTY MAKER

A Blessing for a Neighbour

May the whispers of God's love find you
and settle deep within your heart,
and may each moment be filled
with joy from the start.

May all that you put your hands to
prosper far beyond your dreams,
and may you find grace and sweet gifts,
no matter how bleak things may seem.

May there be a heavenly hovering
over you and the ones you love,
and may you trek along life's path,
being carried, with Help from above.

May you hear Wisdom's voice
when she directs and disciplines,
and may you find peace overflowing
as you surrender to His will yet again.

May you know that I am here to serve and bless you,
however different we may seem,
and may you always know
that we are on the same team.

BLESSING

A Blessing Sung Over You

May the gravity of all that is heavy be lifted
by the light of grace and the weight not felt.

May love anchor you to the wind
and carry you across valleys and to open fields.

May your eyes be wide to the peace
that is gifted in the knowing
that all is well with your soul.

May your hands be open to receive
the roses that are meant for you,
and may their fragrance dance
through the streets you step into.

May the solitude that finds you,
smile in response to what is said there.

May you hear the songs
that God sings over you today,
and feel the warmth of His love as you pray.

May the moon bring to rest
all that still lingers in weight—
for the new day will surely bring
more grace to hold you.

BEAUTY MAKER

A Blessing for the Parent of a Prodigal

May the storm within your heart cease,
knowing that Love's Living Water
has it captured in its stream.

May the wrestle on your life's legacy
bring you across wisdom's threshold
to hope's melody.

May all your regrets be silenced
with the sound of nails,
hammered to take their places.

May you find the words of grace
to always speak Truth
to those who've gone astray.

May your soul dance
to the sweet song of deliverance,
knowing He has a plan.

May all the seeds you've sown,
in quiet faithfulness,
find breath and new growth in Him.

May all that seems lost
rise to the heights of heaven
and redeem all of your thoughts.

And may you know you have a place
in the greatest story ever told—
the story where Beauty saves.

BLESSING

A Blessing for the Persecuted

May You strengthen our brothers and sisters all over the world
when they come against the darkness of today.

May they continue to live in the light of Your love
that has the power to conquer every dark thought,
every ounce of resentment and bitterness from pain,
every persecution that comes their way,
and every retaliation that stems from brokenness.

Let love heal it all.

Help them be brave and courageous,
with a steadfast heart that proclaims,
"Whom else shall I fear if You are for me?"

May their faith carry them from the needs of today
into the miracles of tomorrow.

May the songs of the birds and the flowers of the fields
remind them of the freedom and beauty that is eternal.

If the trek through the sinking mud cannot be removed,
give them strength from heaven,
so they can glide through with a lightness
that only comes from being tied to Your strength
and pulled along by Your grace.

May their hearts know peace,
despite the arrows advancing
and hold a deep knowing that, one day soon,
they will see Your face—everlasting.

BEAUTY MAKER

Hearts Entwined Forever

My heart longed for you
before you were even born.
My heart prayed for you
before you were even formed.

I dreamt of watching you grow up
of singing lullabies to you;
two hearts entwined forever,
watching each other bloom.

Your tiny beating heart,
I never got to hold.
Loved from the very start
but never to grow old.

Your heart needed mine
to get to heaven's door,
and mine needed reminding
where brokenness is restored.

So when I come dancing freely
through heaven's glorious rooms,
I'll thank you for helping me.
Yes darling, my heart needed yours too.

BEAUTY

A Blessing for the Mother in Labour

May the meditations in the breaks between surges
remind you that you can do this,
and may each surge be filled with God's grace
to step through to the next.

May your body do what God intended
and bring new life safely into the world.

May God place the people around you
who need to be there to guide
and give divine wisdom to know
what to do in every moment.

May the waves and moments of pain
tell a testimony of God's goodness.

May His presence be tangible in the room.

May you surrender every fear
to receive what God has for you in this new day,
bringing new life into the world.

May God put breath in your lungs,
strength in your body,
and peace in your spirit.

May you find rest
as you hold the miracle of life
in your arms for the first time,
seeing in this new day together.

You are their mother.

BEAUTY MAKER

A Blessing for the Fathers

May You guide the path he treads
and provide the strength to walk in Truth.
May he always seek to know your ways
as he leads all who live under our roof.

May his legacy reveal eternal fruit
and all that he touches speak of You.
May you surround him with Your angels
and minister to him with Truth.

May he be refreshed in your presence
while hearing the sound of Wisdom's voice.
May You anoint him to lead and love,
always overflowing from the Source.

May You encourage his heart,
spur him on, and give him faith.
May he look to honour You, Father,
and may he see Your glory displayed.

BLESSING

A Blessing for Our Children

Thank You for our children—
for entrusting them to us while they're small.

Pour Your loving grace over their lives,
and may they praise Your name for it all.

Draw their hearts to You daily;
minister to them through every high and low.

Help them to forgive and love,
shining Your light wherever they go.

Provide for their needs,
especially the ones we fail to meet.

Keep their hearts pure—
Guard their minds, and hold their souls.

Guide them towards good company,
and help them discern with whom to share their pearls.

Give them dreams bigger than their own,
and may they always answer Your call.

May they seek Your Word as treasure,
may it direct all of their days.

Soften their hearts towards You,
and may they seek Your wisdom, always.

Protect them from the unseen enemy,
and intercede for them as their lives move.

May they never know a day without Your presence, Lord.
And may they always, always love You.

BEAUTY MAKER

A Blessing for the Anxious Heart

May the thoughts that run away to places you forbid
be brought back to the reality that heaven is on your side.

May you fling open the windows of prayer
and let your sighs find comfort in the One who hears.

May the decisions that weigh heavy on your mind
take a seat and wait their turn.

May the answers you are waiting for
be not rushed as you sit hand in hand with Love.

May the errors you make
take heed of the gift that arrives despite it all.

May you seek truth to fight the lies,
allowing it to battle on your behalf.

May you take a sip of the story that beauty tells
and refuse the cup of bitterness.

May the stars bring you sleep, and, above all,
may your help come from the hills—
not the streets.

This, then, is how you should pray:

"Our Father in heaven, hallowed be your name, your kingdom come, your will be done, on earth as it is in heaven. Give us today our daily bread. And forgive us our debts, as we also have forgiven our debtors. And lead us not into temptation, but deliver us from the evil one."

Matthew 6:9-13 NIV

STORIES

TIMES WHERE I HAVE FOUND GRACE
IN THE LIGHT OF SURRENDER

Unqualified But Chosen

I spilled out all of my mothering insufficiencies to my husband, Ben, one day, explaining that I'm just not patient enough.

I don't have the answers or skills. I don't know if I'm too harsh or too soft. Why would God give me the job of being their mother if I'm not qualified?

Then I was reminded of the very first job I got when I was 14 years old. I got it because I smiled nicely and not much else, I'm sure.

I started with three hours every Saturday at a wedding and formal dress boutique, but I barely spoke to a single customer for weeks. I was meant to greet people as they entered, but I was so timid that I hid behind the racks while straightening and spacing the hangers a very perfect 1 centimetre apart. The store never looked so tidy.

I had a big-hearted boss who loved Jesus, and she saw potential in me. After every shift, we sat down, and she encouraged me, gave me advice, and taught me the skills I lacked. Every time I was in tears due to frustration, embarrassment, or shyness, she prayed with me and believed in me, despite how unqualified I felt at the time. I went on to work there for another nine years. I became their best seller across three stores and even went on to become a store manager.

It was by no accident that God took me to the old car park of this place, my first workplace, now turned gift boutique, to drop off a copy of my very first book, *Fragrant Melodies,* to be stocked in a store. It was another reminder that although I felt unqualified to reach unknown readers in this new written form, I was chosen and called to do it with His help anyway.

So here I am again, tearfully admitting that I clearly don't have all it takes. But God gently reminds me… He chose me for this task for a reason. He is doing a good work, and I will trust Him to complete it.

Perfectly Imperfect

As I look back over my life, I see how the most physically difficult moments I've had were the most influential in directing me to where I am today. The still waters turned into tidal waves, moving me from one place to the next.

I remember as a teenager being bedridden for weeks with no strength to even lift a book or keep my eyes open for more than a few minutes. I called upon God, and He drew near—so very near. He told me in those wearying days to suddenly change my career to a profession that wasn't even on my radar that I had never even heard of at the time.

"Graphic design, God? But what's that?"

The words continued to ring loudly over and over until I surrendered to the path. His voice was kind and loving and full of peace.

I had spent months and months down in the trenches of morning sickness, which had progressively gotten worse with every pregnancy. But in my desperation, I called upon God. He never took away my difficult circumstances or magically helped me handle everything perfectly (a thousand times no). But He drew near, speaking to me in shades I'd never seen before with dreams and visions, one after the other. Then came the physical battle of treading up the steep hills of mothering little ones, and still, I find Him pouring out His grace upon me, even there. His voice is gentle and patient and full of hope.

So I remind myself again, today provides another opportunity to call upon Him. For every day, my circumstances will never be perfectly ideal, the waves always come, and I will often lack the patience I need. But I know that He will show up and turn my ordinary days into moments of communing with Him. Yes, I'll still be imperfect, and my day will still be imperfect. But, when I look up, I will always see this beautiful banner of abundant love stretched out over it all like a rainbow that says, "I promised".

Pockets Full of Truth

All through school, I was one of those kids who had to try really hard to get average grades. I had a go at most things but was never the best at anything. My personality was shy, but I longed to please. I never got subject awards or won age championships. In my final senior year, most of my closest friends got leadership badges, and my best friend got school captain. I didn't. My shy personality just wasn't suited to a leadership position.

But there was one special teacher who saw me when I felt invisible. She knew that I would have been dissapointed in not receiving a leadership badge. She came alongside me and gave me notes and notes of photocopied pages of Bible verses that lived in her pockets once upon a time when she also had to be reminded of God's plans, promises, and who she was in Him. I kept them in mine too. Her encouragement was to make a difference without a leadership badge. I listened.

By the end of year 12, I had received the age champion for athletics and cross country, helped lead my house to win every carnival, received the subject award for hospitality, received the Mentionable Art Award (an honourable art award given in memory of a beloved art teacher to a student exhibiting the same character, enthusiasm, and gifts), the award for Trainee of the Year for the extra study I did at my workplace, and received the school's pastoral care award. All of my chosen subjects were accounted for with an award, and then some.

Right after I had received these awards, I drove my car across the tracks of an approaching train, only metres away, that I didn't see until it was almost too late. I nearly finished my race that night, but God still had more ground for me to tread.

Following Jesus often feels like that—all this work for years on end, often with nothing to show for it, no special title, and despite many limitations of abilities and personality. We won't see all the ripples we make in this life until the final ceremony. But in the meantime, take heed of the faith that was once planted in me. You can make a difference where you are without the badge. Just be sure to fill your pockets with Truth and count every day that you live as a gift.

My frame was not hidden from you when I was made in the secret place, when I was woven together in the depths of the earth. Your eyes saw my unformed body; all the days ordained for me were written in your book before one of them came to be.

Psalms 139:15-16 NIV

Redeeming a Broken Heart

Before the birth of our first child, we waited and prayed. We tried all the things and then surrendered all the things, while still praying and trying. Even after all of the pain and disappointment, my heart still knew God was good, but I remember weeping on my knees and singing my song of lament. It was a fragrant song, a faith song, but it had a sadness. After five years of waiting and choosing to worship God through it all, our fragrant flower, Jasmine, was born—the beginning of a new song of praise.

A few years later, we were given another gift; we named him Isaac, meaning laughter. The year after he was born was hard. He wasn't a straightforward baby because of a misdiagnosed and overlooked lip and tongue tie. He struggled to feed and therefore wasn't happy when he was awake and struggled to sleep for the first 6 months of his life until I got a second opinion on his ties and got them corrected. I had to fight hard to keep my joy, but because of this it now runs much deeper.

A few years later, we were given Henry, meaning, 'hero'. A hero is known for his boldness, fighting for others, and bringing peace. The year after he was born, I found a new passion to fight for these things through writing and telling my testimonies of God's goodness.

Then I fell pregnant with baby number four. The morning that brought the news also brought a quiet whisper that said it was to be a girl called Lucy Grace, meaning 'bringer of light.' The same quiet (but also mysteriously loud) voice confirmed again and again that my testimonies were to be brought into the light for the benefit of others.

And, by God's grace, *Fragrant Melodies* was birthed.

Throughout the 9 months of growing Lucy, sunflowers stood out to me. Their light-filled faces spoke to me of a 'sunny bloom' about to spring up in the night, and I wrote a poem about it (page 114). The night that I went into labour, I walked into the room where I would soon hold my baby in my arms, still unsure whether the whispers I had heard were all just a miraculous mirage. But when I saw the large painting of sunflowers hanging on the wall in the labour suite, I knew.

I later discovered that my midwife's name, Saffron, also meant 'yellow flower' and is a fragrant spice harvested from the stamen of a purple crocus, a flower I admire for its longevity in drought and optimism after rain. Lucy Grace was born as the first light of dawn streamed through the window and onto the painting of sunflowers and her little face.

Both Ben and I, after seeking the Lord, felt that God wanted to add baby number 5 to our family. We knew that being obedient to God's voice meant that we would be met with the grace to walk the path, whatever it might hold. So, we here we are, with Noah as our sweet fifth child. My grandma tells me that the number five is actually the number of God's grace. I continue to cling to His mercy and loving-kindness, just as Noah did, as I build what He tells me to build and pray for fresh outpourings of His beautiful grace as people surrender their hearts to Him.

Each of our children have their own stories of God's glory to grow into, but how beautiful that we are all woven together in this shimmering tapestry of life.

Hindsight has given me the gift of seeing how God brought me through the grief I felt—all those years that I felt I'd lost, the questions of God's faithfulness, the pain I felt in the waiting, the doubts I had through it all.

God gave me the specific tools and the divine help I needed that aligned with my personality and gifts to move through to the other side so that my grief did not become bitterness that choked my seeds of faith. I have seen His golden fingerprints of glory redeem the time of infertility in ways I never thought possible.

I can't help but keep sharing the goodness of God, who I know makes everything beautiful in His time. My cup overflows.

ACKNOWLEDGMENTS

This book exists with grateful thanks to:

My lover and friend, Ben.

Our story is no ordinary story. The way we met was no coincidence. I thank God that we have each other, traveling along this path that He has set before us.

This book is an echo of the prayer that we wrote on the front of each engagement invitation:

"Let this be our destiny, to share our lives together so that we may with one voice glorify God."

That was always our prayer.

You have shown me what it means to live a life of surrender, putting yourself aside to serve your family in love. You continue to be steadfast, dependable, and faithful.

Thank you for indulging in my poetic side and encouraging my gifts and creativity.

Thank you, and I love you.

My five children: Jasmine, Isaac, Henry, Lucy, and Noah.

You are our little seeds who we keep watering and trusting and praying that God will make a beautiful harvest from.

May your cups overflow with grace, in the light of surrender as you sojourn here, before God calls you home.

www.ingramcontent.com/pod-product-compliance
Lightning Source LLC
Chambersburg PA
CBHW060353110426
42743CB00036B/2832